Netherland

Travel Guide 2024

Your Perfect Travel Partner For An Intimate
Tour of the Netherland in 2024

Florence Whitehead

Table of Contents

Map of Central Netherland

Introduction

Welcome to the Netherlands, a captivating country in northwestern Europe, often referred to as Holland. Renowned for its low-lying terrain, the name "Netherlands" itself translates to a low-lying country. The nation embraces a parliamentary democracy under a constitutional monarch, with Amsterdam as its vibrant capital and The Hague as the seat of government.

With its remarkable flatness, the Dutch landscape features expansive lakes, rivers, and canals. Over 2,500 square miles have been reclaimed through meticulous water management dating back to medieval times. Windmills, exemplified by the UNESCO World Heritage Site Kinderdijk-Elshout, played a pivotal role in this land reclamation, replacing earlier manual efforts.

Despite significant post-World War II emigration, the Netherlands stands as one of the world's most densely populated countries. Amsterdam, a hub of international youth culture, reflects the Dutch tradition of social tolerance, evident in legalized practices such as prostitution, soft-drug use, and euthanasia. The Netherlands, a pioneer in social progress, notably legalized same-sex marriage.

Historically, the Dutch displayed an independent outlook, rejecting monarchical controls in the 16th and 17th centuries. The nation's advanced economy persisted through the centuries, fostering international cooperation. As a member of the EU and NATO, the Netherlands hosts various international organizations, including the International Court of Justice.

However, the Dutch reputation for tolerance faced challenges in the late 20th and early 21st centuries, marked by growing nationalism and xenophobia amid increased immigration. The country is geographically vulnerable, with a significant portion lying below sea level, protected by dunes and dikes.

Explore the Netherlands' diverse terrain, from the flat polders to the elevated eastern region, home to the Hoge Veluwe National Park. Experience the unique geography, where a significant part of the country rests just above sea level, creating a distinctive and resilient Dutch landscape.

Discover the intriguing history of the Zuiderzee, once an estuary of the Rhine River. Transformed by natural forces into a shallow inland sea, it took on an almost circular shape due to winds and tides. The Zuiderzee project, initiated in 1920, led to the construction of the IJsselmeer Dam (Afsluitdijk), sealing off the Zuiderzee in 1932. This 19-mile-long dam created the IJsselmeer Lake and the IJsselmeer Polders, covering 650 square miles, and was utilized for agriculture and diverse purposes like residential and industrial development.

In the southwest, the 1953 gales and tide disaster accelerated the Delta Project, constructing dams and bridges to combat sea inlets, reduce coastline, and facilitate development. The unique landscape formed by the Rhine, Lek, Waal, and Maas rivers in the central region showcases high dikes, orchards, and large bridges connecting the central and southern provinces.

During the Pleistocene Epoch, the Scandinavian ice sheet covered the north, leaving moraine. The Holocene Epoch saw the deposition of clay and the creation of lakes, some of which were reclaimed in later centuries. The Netherlands experiences a temperate climate with gentle winters, cool summers, and rainfall throughout the year. The country's geographical position results in weather influenced by warm and polar air masses colliding.

Explore the diverse plant and animal life shaped by the Atlantic district within the Euro-Siberian phytogeographic region. The Netherlands boasts a variety of landscapes, from coastal sand dunes to woods and heaths.

Wildlife, including seabirds, migrating birds, and larger mammals, is found in nature reserves like the Naardermeer, Hoge Veluwe National Park, and Oostvaardersplassen. Embark on a journey through the Netherlands' captivating geography, where history and nature intersect to create a dynamic and resilient landscape.

Chapter One

Planning Your Journey

A.Optimal Timing for Your Visit

There are various compelling reasons to explore the Netherlands, whether it's witnessing the vibrant tulip blooms, participating in Amsterdam's lively King's Day celebrations, or leisurely cycling along picturesque dykes and canals. To make the most of your visit, consider factors like weather, crowd levels, and your budget.

- Here's a comprehensive guide to help you plan the perfect time for your Netherlands adventure.

High Season: June to August

The best time to go for decent weather

Expect bustling crowds, higher prices, and early accommodation bookings.

Ideal for enjoying balmy weather, outdoor cafés, and countryside bike rides.

April to May and September to October are shoulder seasons.

The best time to go for moderate prices

Experience fewer crowds, moderate prices, and open attractions.

The weather can be wet, so bring warm clothes for outdoor activities.

Low Season: November to March

Best time to go to avoid crowds

Cities are quieter, making them perfect for museum visits.

Outside cities, some sights close during the winter, and the weather can be chilly.

Monthly Highlights:

- January

Cold and dark, but museums have fewer visitors.

National Tulip Day kicks off the annual tulip season.

- February

Still cold, but southern provinces gear up for Carnival celebrations.

Amsterdam International Fashion Week takes place.

- March

Visit Keukenhof Gardens for early bulb field viewing.

TEFAF, Europe's largest art show, takes place in Maastricht.

- April

King's Day celebrations dominate, especially in Amsterdam.

A World Press Photo event occurs.

- May

Explore post-King's Day with changing weather.

Herdenkingsdag & Bevrijdingsdag (Remembrance Day and Liberation Day) vinden plaats.

- June

The summer peak season begins with numerous events.

Ideal weather for outdoor activities, festivals, and bicycle rides.

- July

Long days, sunshine, and bustling beaches. Events include Keti Koti, North Sea Jazz Festival, and De Vierdaagse.

- August

Pleasant temperatures are milder than in other European hot spots.

Events like Pride Amsterdam and Sneekweek occur.

- September

Superb festivals, fair weather, and fewer crowds.

Key events include Wereldhavendagen and the Nederlands Film Festival.

- October

Autumn colors, mild weather, and lower prices. Events include Leidens Ontzet and the Amsterdam Dance Event.

- November

Cultural events, reduced rates, and festive preparations.

Events include Glow and the International Documentary Film Festival.

- December

Winter magic, holiday traditions, and New Year's Eve celebrations.

Key events include Sinterklaas, Christmas Day, and New Year's Eve festivities.

B.Visa Requirements and Travel Documentation

For your journey to the Netherlands, understanding visa requirements and having the right travel documentation are crucial. This thorough guide will assist you in navigating the process:

- Determining Visa Need:

Check whether your nationality and planned stay duration require a Dutch visa.

Explore this link to verify your specific visa requirements.

- Visa Application Process:

Make an appointment at the local Dutch consulate or embassy.

Present the necessary documents in Dutch, English, French, or Spanish.

- Key documents needed:

Completed and signed Netherlands visa application form, available on the embassy's website.

Recent passport pictures meeting specified criteria.

Valid passport or travel documentation, not older than 10 years, with at least 2 empty visa pages.

Copies of the passport's personal details and previous passports' pages.

Copies of previous visas with entry/exit stamps.

Evidence of legal residence in your current country.

Complete travel itinerary, including reservations to and from the Schengen area (not an airplane ticket).

Proof of return plans, like an employment contract, employer declaration, school enrollment, or property ownership document. Netherlands Schengen visa health insurance with coverage of at least €30,000.

Additional Requirements Based on the Applicant's Status:

- Employed:

Payslips from the last three months.

Employment contract.

Approved leave of absence from the employer.

- Self-employed:

Company's certificate of registration.

- Retired:

Pension statements from the past three months.

Proof of income from business or property ownership.

- Sponsored:

Proof of sponsorship and/or private accommodation.

- Financial Means:

Proof of sufficient funds: at least €34 per person per day for the entire stay.

Proof of income for the sponsor.

- For Minors:

Extract of the minor's birth certificate.

Identity documents with both parents' signatures.

Declaration of consent from both parents.

Possibly, a court statement on custody or a school declaration.

- For the Caribbean part of the Kingdom:

Requirements are similar to those of a regular short-stay visa.

Potential differences may include a specific travel insurance amount, copies of all passport pages, and a residence permit for foreign applicants.

Ensure all documents are meticulously prepared, attend your appointment, and stay informed about the latest travel regulations. For personalized guidance, contact the Dutch embassy or consulate in your area.

C. Crafting Your Budget

Crafting a budget for your Netherlands trip involves considering various factors. Here's a breakdown to help you plan your finances:

- Daily Budget:

Mid-range budget: $152 per person per day.

Couples: $1,926 per week.

Solo Traveler: $1,063 per week.

- Flight Prices:

From Chile to Amsterdam: starting at $1,455.

From the United Kingdom to Amsterdam: starting at $75.

- Accommodation:

Hostels: Average $50 per night for a bed in a shared dorm.

Hotels: Around $145 per night for a double room.

Airbnb: average $144 for a private room.

- Daily food costs:

Budget $40 per day per person for meals (breakfast, lunch, and dinner).

Consider takeout or food tours for variety.

- Food prices in the Netherlands:

Sandwich with a soft drink: $8.

Bitterballen (deep-fried snacks): $7.

Stroopwafels (local biscuits): $4.

Bottle of water: $1.60.

Three-course meal with a glass of wine in a high-end restaurant: $65.

Steak dinner with a glass of wine: $48.

- Local Transportation:

Public transportation using the OV Chipkaart:

1-day pass: $9.65.

7-day pass: $44.

Single ticket: $3.43 (valid for one hour).

- Train tickets (one-way):

Amsterdam naar Utrecht: $10.60.

Amsterdam to Leiden: $12.54.

Amsterdam to Maastricht: $32.60.

Amsterdam to The Hague: $15.54.

- Bike Rental:

Dutch bike (3 hours): $10.

City bike (3 hours): $13.

- Car Rental:

Approximately $60 per day.

Consider road trips for countryside exploration.

- Attractions:

Anne Frank House:

Adult ticket: $18.

Child ticket: $9.

- Van Gogh Museum:

Adult ticket: $21.

Child: Free.

ThanksRembrandt House:

Adult ticket: $18.

Child ticket: $6.

- Rijksmuseum:

Adult ticket: $32.

Child: Free.

Remember to factor in sightseeing expenses, and check out more details in our ultimate Netherlands travel guide for additional insights into weather, traditional food, and recommended cities to explore. Happy planning!

D.Efficient Transportation Tips

Navigating the Netherlands is a breeze due to its compact size and efficient transportation systems. Here are some pointers for navigating:

By Train:

- Preferred Mode: Trains are the best way to travel. Operated by Nederlandse Spoorwegen (NS), they are fast, frequent, and punctual.
- Ticketing: Buy tickets in advance, and remember that tickets can't be purchased on trains.
- Fares and Discounts: Fares are calculated by distance. Consider discount options like Dagkaart (Day

Travel Card) or Weekendretour (Weekend Return).

By bus and tram:

- Complementing Trains: Buses supplement train routes, reaching even remote areas.
- Ticketing: Pay the driver or use an OV-chipkaart for seamless travel.
- Urban Transport: Major towns have extensive and affordable urban public transport systems.

By Car:

- Smooth Driving: Roads are well-maintained, and driving is generally smooth.
- Rules of the Road: Drive on the right, adhere to speed limits, and wear seat belts.
- Fuel and Toll: There are no toll roads, but fuel is relatively expensive.

Renting a car:

- Requirements: Drivers must be 21 or older and have a credit card.
- Insurance: Adequate insurance is essential, and breakdown coverage is advisable.
- Rental Charges: Prices start around €250 per week, including a collision damage waiver.

Cycling:

- Cycle-Touring: Explore the Netherlands effortlessly by bike due to its flat landscape.
- Cycle Paths: Well-marked cycle paths make cycling safe and enjoyable.
- Bike Rental: Rent bikes from train stations or local shops; prices vary, and reservations are recommended.
- Taking Bikes on Trains: Allowed with a flat-rate ticket; restrictions during rush hours.

Treintaxi Scheme:

- Rail Passengers: Treintaxi offers taxi services to and from about thirty train stations in the NS network.
- Booking: Call in advance for station-to-home journeys within city limits.

Efficient public transport:

- Integrated Network: The Netherlands boasts an integrated network of trains, buses, and trams.
- Wide Reach: Even the smallest villages are easily accessible.
- Local Timetables: Check local bus timetables, especially in remote areas where advance bookings may be necessary.

Cautions for Cyclists:

- Bike Theft: Lock your bike securely, as bike theft is prevalent.
- Onboard NS Trains: Purchase a flat-rate ticket for €6 for your bike; restrictions during rush hours.

Efficiency and ease characterize transportation in the Netherlands, making it convenient for both tourists and locals alike. Enjoy your travels!

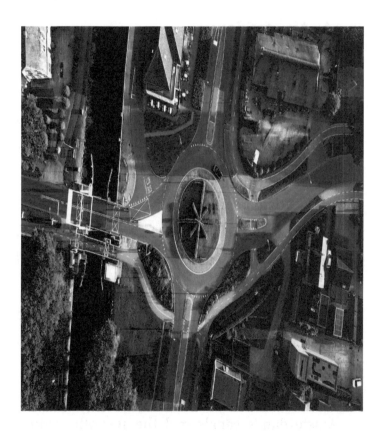

Chapter Two

Vibrant Destinations

A. Amsterdam

Amsterdam, often dubbed the "Venice of the North," is the capital and largest city of the Netherlands. Renowned for its picturesque canals, the city has a rich history and a vibrant modern character. Here are some key aspects:

- History and Origins:

Founded at the mouth of the Amstel River, Amsterdam's name stems from a local linguistic variation of the word "dam."

Originating as a fishing village, it flourished into a major world port during the Dutch Golden Age in the 17th century.

- UNESCO World Heritage:

Amsterdam's canals and the 19-20th century Defence Line are designated UNESCO World Heritage Sites.

- Cultural Hub:

Home to cultural landmarks like the Rijksmuseum, Van Gogh Museum, and Anne Frank House.

Known for openness, liberalism, and tolerance, reflecting its long tradition.

- Financial and Commercial Center:

Hosts the historic Amsterdam Stock Exchange, considered the world's oldest "modern" securities market.

A major financial center with the headquarters of notable companies like Philips, AkzoNobel, and ING.

- Global City:

Recognized as an alpha world city with a significant role in finance, culture, and technology.

Hosts the European headquarters of leading tech companies like Uber, Netflix, and Tesla.

- Quality of Living:

Ranked 9th globally as the best city to live in by the Economist Intelligence Unit in 2022.

Scores well on quality of living for environment and infrastructure.

- Multicultural and Diverse:

Known for its multiculturalism, boasting representation from at least 177 nationalities. Current challenges include immigration and ethnic segregation.

- Transportation Hub:

Houses the busy Schiphol Airport, the third busiest in Europe.

The Port of Amsterdam ranks as the fifth largest in Europe.

- Notable Residents:

Throughout history, notable figures like Rembrandt, Vincent van Gogh, and philosopher Baruch Spinoza have called Amsterdam home.

Amsterdam's unique blend of history, cultural richness, and modern dynamism makes it a vibrant destination drawing millions of visitors each year.

1.Canal Cruises and Cityscape Delights

- Canal Cruises:

Embark on a unique journey through the Netherlands with enchanting canal cruises, providing a special glimpse into the country's history and landscapes.

- Amsterdam Canals:

Explore the iconic canals of Amsterdam, often hailed as the "Venice of the North."

Glide past 17th-century canal houses, historic bridges, and vibrant markets.

Choose from diverse canal tour options, including daytime, evening, and themed cruises.

- Utrecht Waterways:

Delight in the serenity of Utrecht's canals, adorned with medieval wharfs and lively cafes.

Experience unique views of Utrecht's Dom Tower and architectural gems.

- Rotterdam Harbor Tours:

Discover Rotterdam's modern allure with harbor cruises showcasing innovative architecture and maritime landscapes.

Witness the juxtaposition of contemporary designs and historic port areas.

- Cityscape Delights:

Immerse yourself in the captivating cityscapes where Dutch urban centers blend historic charm with modern innovation.

- Amsterdam's Historic Center:

Wander through the cobbled streets of Amsterdam's historic center, featuring landmarks like Dam Square and the Royal Palace.

Enjoy a mix of traditional Dutch architecture and lively street life.

- Utrecht's Old Town:

Stroll through Utrecht's charming old town, characterized by medieval canals, lively squares, and the iconic Dom Tower.

Explore cultural attractions, boutique shops, and cozy cafes.

- Rotterdam's Architectural Marvels:

Experience Rotterdam's cutting-edge architecture, including the Cube Houses and Erasmus Bridge.

Discover the city's cultural scene with museums, galleries, and waterfront dining.

- Canal-Side Dining and Entertainment:

Indulge in canal-side dining, savoring Dutch cuisine while enjoying scenic views.

Experience vibrant nightlife along the canals with bars, clubs, and live music venues.

Whether navigating historic canals or exploring cityscapes, Netherlands' canal cruises and city delights offer a harmonious blend of tradition and modernity, promising a memorable journey through this captivating European destination.

2.Cultural hotspots

- The Rijksmuseum:

Magnificent after extensive refurbishment, showcasing a world-famous collection of Old Masters.

Expect crowds, especially around masterpieces like Rembrandt's Night Watch.

Explore less congested areas like the Asian Pavilion and special collections.

- Stedelijk Gallery:

Modern Art gallery with a major facelift and controversial architectural extension.

Improved visitor experience, featuring new galleries and impressive exhibitions.

Summer exhibitions include striking works by artist Jeff Wall and an extraordinary exhibition by Dutch designer Marcel Wanders.

- Film EYE:

Blend of cinema and media gallery with striking white architecture on the Amsterdam waterfront.

Current exhibition "Cinema Remake Art and Film" features filmmakers and artists creating new works from existing films.

Offers an impressive film program and a great café with waterfront views.

- The Hermitage Amsterdam:

Dutch spin-off of the St. Petersburg museum with changing exhibitions.

The Silk Road exhibition showcases objects and art, but some find it object-focused.

Housed in the historic Amstelhof, a quieter alternative to crowded attractions.

- Het Scheepvaart – Maritime Museum:

Engaging museum for all ages, featuring nautical history, figureheads, and interactive displays.

Replica of Dutch East Indies ship "The Amsterdam" provides a glimpse into the 18th Century maritime life.

Modernization of the museum offers an interactive and entertaining experience.

- Finding NEMO:

Interactive Science Center designed by architect Renzo Piano, resembling an ocean liner.

Offers hands-on activities for kids and breathtaking views of the port of Amsterdam.

A striking addition to the Amsterdam waterfront.

- Van Gogh Museum:

The House has one of the best collections of Van Gogh's oil paintings, drawings, and personal letters.

Changing exhibitions add variety to the experience.

Currently featuring the works of Franco-Swiss artist Felix Vallotton.

- Anne Frank's House and Jordaan Neighborhood:

Iconic house where Anne Frank wrote her diary during WWII; book ahead or visit during the late-night opening.

Explore the scenic Jordaan area with quirky shops, cafes, and canal-side houses.

Amsterdam's changing waterfront: Take a ferry ride from Central Station for a different perspective on the city; explore the arty-eco quarter at NDSM Werf.

Amsterdam offers a rich cultural experience with revamped museums, iconic galleries, and unique perspectives on its historic and modern facets.

3.Iconic Museums and Historical Gems

Iconic Museums:

- Rijksmuseum, Amsterdam:

Home to Dutch masterpieces by Rembrandt, Vermeer, and Frans Hals.

Spans over 800 years of Dutch art and history, showcasing paintings, sculptures, ceramics, and more.

- Van Gogh Museum, Amsterdam:
Dedicated to Vincent van Gogh's works, featuring over 200 paintings, drawings, and letters.

Highlights include masterpieces like "The Starry Night" and "Sunflowers."

- Mauritshuis, The Hague:
Housed in a 17th-century palace, displaying Dutch Golden Age paintings by Vermeer, Rembrandt, and Jan Steen.

Features iconic pieces like Vermeer's "Girl with a Pearl Earring" and Rembrandt's "The Anatomy Lesson of Dr. Nicolaes Tulp."

- Stedelijk Museum, Amsterdam:
Amsterdam's key modern and contemporary art museum, spanning the 19th and 21st centuries.

Exhibits works by influential artists such as Picasso, Matisse, and Mondrian.

- Kröller-Müller Museum, Otterlo:
Hidden gem in Hoge Veluwe National Park, dedicated to Vincent van Gogh's art.

Offers an extensive collection of paintings, drawings, and letters in a serene parkland setting.

- Anne Frank Museum, Amsterdam:

Located in the building where Anne Frank hid during WWII, preserving her legacy.

Features the secret annex and exhibitions on Anne's life and the Holocaust.

- Discover the museums in the Netherlands:

Whether you're an art enthusiast or seeking a fun day out, the Netherlands' museums offer diverse collections and exhibitions.

Historical Gems:

- Anne Frank House, Amsterdam:

Museum preserving Anne Frank's hiding place during WWII, offering insight into wartime history.

- Rijksmuseum, Amsterdam:

Immersive experience in Dutch art and history, housing masterpieces by Rembrandt and Vermeer.

- Van Gogh Museum, Amsterdam: World's largest collection of Van Gogh's works, tracing the artist's evolution and impact.
- Keukenhof Gardens, Lisse: Breathtaking tulip and flower gardens, among the world's largest, offer a visual feast.
- Kinderdijk Windmills: UNESCO-listed windmills showcase Dutch water management ingenuity.
- Dom Tower, Utrecht: Tallest church tower in the Netherlands, providing panoramic views of Utrecht.
- Zaanse Schans, Zaandam: Open-air museum with historic windmills, traditional houses, and artisan workshops.
- Mauritshuis, The Hague: 17th-century mansion housing a remarkable collection of Dutch Golden Age paintings.
- Delft's Old Town: This charming town is known for its historic market square, medieval buildings, and iconic blue pottery.

- Medieval Castle De Haar, Utrecht:
Fairytale-like castle with lush gardens, restored in the late 19th century.
- Maastricht Underground Caves:
a vast network of underground caves and tunnels with a rich history.
- St. Bavo's Church, Haarlem:
Impressive church architecture with the famous Müller organ in Haarlem.

From art and architecture to natural wonders and historic sites, the Netherlands offers a diverse array of historical gems, each contributing to its rich cultural heritage.

B.Keukenhof Gardens and the Tulip Fields:

- Keukenhof Gardens in Holland:
Open from March 21 to May 12, 2024, offering a splendid tulip experience near Amsterdam.
Over 7 million flower bulbs were planted by hand, featuring 800 different tulip varieties.

Celebrating its 75th anniversary in 2024 with an extra festive edition.

- Keukenhof Theme 2024:

The park is dedicated to a yearly theme, with gardens, events, and artworks aligned.

The 2024 theme for Keukenhof's 75th anniversary is yet to be revealed.

- Walking Between the Tulips:

32 hectares of flower-filled landscapes with 10 miles of hiking trails.

Weekly changing flower shows, ponds, pavilions, and diverse restaurants for a scenic stroll.

Largest statue garden in the Netherlands, showcasing works by national and international artists.

- Visit Keukenhof with children:

Family-friendly with treasure hunts, a petting zoo, maze, and playground.

Miffy playground for the little ones, providing an enjoyable day out for all.

- Keukenhof Park Guide Book:

Order the guide book for a behind-the-scenes glimpse and a souvenir of your visit.

Available for €7.00, pick up at the entrance with your online ticket.

When should I visit Keukenhof?

Open from March 21 to May 12, 2024, with three flowering periods.

Early blooming flowers, indoor shows with tulips, daffodils, and crocuses.

Hyacinths and early tulips bloom in outdoor gardens, creating vibrant indoor shows.

Main tulip blooms outdoors, green trees, and ongoing indoor flower shows.

- Opening Hours, Keukenhof:

Open daily from 08:00 to 19:30 (March 21 to May 12, 2024).

- Price Keukenhof Gardens:

Tickets for €23.00 are available online in advance.

Limited tickets are available at the box office; booking online is recommended.

Select a day and time slot for entry due to the maximum number of tickets per day.

Note:

On busy days, Keukenhof may be sold out; consider combination tickets with the Keukenhof bus or tours from Amsterdam for more availability.

How to travel to Keukenhof:

Keukenhof Gardens is conveniently located near Amsterdam, Amsterdam Airport Schiphol, and other Dutch cities such as Haarlem, Leiden, The Hague, Rotterdam, and Delft. Plan your trip in advance with various travel options:

- Public Transport:

Utilize the Keukenhof Bus Express for easy access to the flower park.

- Car:

Drive to the flower park by car, providing flexibility in your journey.

Guided Tours:

Book guided tours from Amsterdam, The Hague, or Rotterdam for a seamless experience.

- Taxi:

For a convenient and comfortable ride, choose a taxi service.

- Biking or walking:

Explore Keukenhof Gardens by biking or walking, enjoying the scenic surroundings.

- Events at Keukenhof:

Regular events enhance the experience; check the schedule for special occasions during your visit.

Notable events in 2024:

- March 21-24: Opening Weekend
- March 29–April 1: Easter Weekend
- April 6-7: Holland Heritage Weekend
- April 20: Keukenhof Flower Parade
- April 27: King's Day
- April 27–May 5: May Holiday
- May 9: Ascension Day and Weekend
- May 11–12: Romance at Keukenhof (Mother's Day)

Experience the Tulip Fields Around Keukenhof:

- Boat Trip:

Take a boat trip to Keukenhof to view tulip fields from the water (separate from the Keukenhof ticket).

- Cycling:

Discover tulip fields by bike; Keukenhof offers cycle routes with rentals available.

- Sightseeing Tours:

Explore tulip fields with an electric Renault Twizy, an electric scooter, a tuktuk private tour, or a helicopter flight.

- Hotels near Keukenhof:

Consider staying overnight for an early visit; nearby hotels often offer more affordable options than those in Amsterdam.

- Keukenhof Address:

Keukenhof Tulip Gardens, Stationsweg 166a, 2161 AM Lisse, Phone: +31 252 465555

1.Blossoming Beauty:

The Tulip Legacy: From Mania to Marvel
Dutch tulip affection is rooted in the 17th-century Tulip Mania, evolving into a symbol of wealth.

Today, the Netherlands stands as the world's largest tulip producer, embracing tulip season.

Keukenhof Gardens: A Floral Extravaganza
Keukenhof, "The Garden of Europe," in Lisse, showcases over seven million bulbs, creating a sensory delight.

Themed displays, historic Keukenhof Castle, and vibrant flower arrangements offer a unique experience.

Tulip Fields of Noordoostpolder: A Technicolor Dream
The reclaimed Noordoostpolder region transforms into extensive tulip fields, a surreal canvas of colors.

Sunrise or sunset visits provide magical lighting for photography and appreciation of the fields' beauty.

Floral Parade: Bloemencorso:

The Bloemencorso, or Flower Parade, is an annual tradition showcasing artistically decorated floats.

Floats adorned with tulips, daffodils, and hyacinths parade through the streets, creating a moving masterpiece.

2.Seasonal Floral Spectacles:

- Keukenhof Gardens (Spring):

Witness the renowned tulip displays in Keukenhof Gardens, a vibrant celebration of color and floral diversity.

- Flower Fields of Lisse (Spring):

Explore the vast flower fields around Lisse, featuring tulips, daffodils, and hyacinths in a stunning mosaic.

- Amsterdam Flower Market (Spring):

Experience the lively Amsterdam Flower Market, a bustling hub offering a variety of flowers, bulbs, and plants.

- Dahlia Gardens in Zundert (late summer):

Visit the Dahlia Gardens in Zundert during late summer, which showcase intricate designs and vibrant dahlia colors.

- Dutch Orchid Greenhouses (year-round):

Tour Dutch orchid greenhouses year-round to witness the cultivation of exotic and diverse orchid species.

- Aalsmeer Flower Auction (year-round):

Explore the Aalsmeer Flower Auction, one of the world's largest, and observe the bustling trade of floral masterpieces.

- Dutch Rose Gardens (Summer):

Discover enchanting rose gardens across the country, with various rose species in full bloom during the summer.

- Lavender Fields in Limburg (Summer):

Enjoy the aromatic beauty of Limburg's lavender fields, which create a picturesque landscape in the summer.

- Hortus botanicus, Leiden (year-round): Visit the Hortus Botanicus in Leiden to explore a diverse collection of plants and flowers in a historic botanical garden.
  - Amstelpark Rose Garden, Amsterdam (Summer):
Stroll through the serene Amstelpark Rose Garden in Amsterdam, featuring a stunning display of roses.
  - Holland Dahlia Festival, Zundert (Late Summer):
Attend the Holland Dahlia Festival in Zundert, where elaborate dahlia floats parade through the streets.
  - Floral Parade of Aalsmeer (Spring):
Experience the vibrant Floral Parade of Aalsmeer, featuring elaborately decorated floats adorned with flowers.

3.Horticultural Wonders

Keukenhof Gardens: Lisse, Netherlands
In the Dutch town of Lisse, Keukenhof Gardens unveils a breathtaking display of over 7 million bulbs during spring, featuring tulips, crocuses, hyacinths, and daffodils. Originally designed in 1949, the gardens showcase Holland's hybrid blooms and host themed shows in six glass pavilions.

Hortus botanicus Leiden: Leiden, Netherlands
Established in 1590, Hortus Botanicus Leiden is the oldest botanical garden in the Netherlands. Founded by botanist Carolus Clusius, it houses over 10,000 plant species and plays a vital role in research, preservation, and horticultural education.

Green Cathedral: Almere, Netherlands
The Green Cathedral near Almere, conceived by Marinus Boezem, is a living land art project featuring 178 poplars arranged to mimic the architecture of Notre-Dame de Reims. This

unique creation serves as both a venue for weddings and funerals.

Pinetum Blijdenstein: Hilversum, Netherlands

Hidden behind enchanting walls, Pinetum Blijdenstein in Hilversum boasts one of the world's most comprehensive collections of gymnosperms. This botanical gem, part of the Dutch National Plant Collection, contributes to biodiversity preservation and offers a serene setting for visitors.

These horticultural wonders, from the historic Keukenhof Gardens to the serene Hortus Botanicus Leiden, the artistic Green Cathedral, and the diverse Pinetum Blijdenstein, showcase the Netherlands' deep-rooted connection with nature and its commitment to preserving botanical diversity.

Hortus botanicus Leiden: Leiden, Netherlands

Established in 1590, Hortus Botanicus Leiden stands as the oldest botanical garden in the Netherlands. Founded by pioneering botanist

Carolus Clusius, it originated less than 50 years after the Botanical Garden of Pisa, holding a Guinness World Record for being the oldest botanical garden. Today, it shelters over 10,000 plant species from around the globe in its beds and greenhouses. Notable for its carnivorous plant collection and impressive cycads, it serves as a living museum and a haven for students.

Green Cathedral: Almere, Netherlands

Emulating the grandeur of the Cathedral of Notre-Dame de Reims, the Green Cathedral near Almere, Netherlands, is an artful creation by Marinus Boezem. Comprising 178 strategically-planted Lombardy poplars, this living land art project stretches almost 100 feet into the sky and spans nearly 500 feet by 246 feet. A venue for weddings and funerals, the Green Cathedral is designed for its own organic evolution, with poplars giving way to beech trees, shaping the green church's walls anew.

C.Utrecht:

Historic Charm on the Oudegracht

Utrecht, the fourth-largest city in the Netherlands, boasts a historic city center with structures dating back to the High Middle Ages. At its heart lies the Oudegracht, a canal featuring vibrant terraces, historic wharfs, and concealed cellars. Once the religious center of the Netherlands, Utrecht played a pivotal role in shaping the Dutch Republic. While Amsterdam later took the cultural spotlight during the Dutch Golden Age, Utrecht remained significant, housing the largest university in the Netherlands and serving as a central hub for transportation.

1.Historic Charm:

Amsterdam's Canal Ring: UNESCO-listed, 17th-century buildings, and charming houseboats define Amsterdam's Canal Ring.

Leiden's Old Town: Cobblestone pathways lead to picturesque canals, courtyards, and historic landmarks in Leiden.

Haarlem's Grote Markt: Experience the lively atmosphere surrounded by medieval buildings and St. Bavo's Church.

Delft's Market Square: Stroll through historic buildings, cafes, and the Nieuwe Kerk in Delft's Markt Square.

Zaanse Schans Windmills: Step back in time at this open-air museum with well-preserved historic windmills.

Kampen's Medieval Architecture: Admire well-preserved medieval architecture, including city gates and the Church of St. Nicholas in Kampen.

Gouda's Market Square: Explore the medieval ambiance, home to the historic town hall and the renowned Gouda Cheese Market.

Maastricht's Vrijthof Square: Enjoy the historic beauty surrounded by churches, cafes, and charming cobblestone streets.

Amersfoort's Koppelpoort: Marvel at the well-preserved medieval city gate, offering a glimpse into Amersfoort's past.

Enkhuizens Zuiderzee Museum: Visit the outdoor museum showcasing traditional Dutch houses, shops, and maritime heritage.

Naarden's Fortifications: Discover the star-shaped fortifications of Naarden, a historic town with well-preserved walls, bastions, and a moat.

The Netherlands"cities and towns weave historic charm into their fabric, creating an enchanting atmosphere reminiscent of bygone eras.

2. Unique Cafés and Shops

- Sweet Cup, Amsterdam:

Nestled near Leidseplein, Sweet Cup stands out as a micro-coffee bar and roastery in Amsterdam. This charming spot is known for its outstanding coffee, notably the award-winning Kenya blend. The café's unpretentious atmosphere, along with the presence of Sjefke, the resident basset hound, adds to its allure. Whether you're seeking excellent cappuccinos or premium beans for home brewing, Sweet Cup is a gem among Amsterdam's artisanal coffee scene.

Other great places in Amsterdam are Two For Joy, Caffeination, Lot Sixty One, Quartier Putain, and Espressofabriek.

- Man Met Bril Koffie, Rotterdam:

Founded by Paul Sharo, this Rotterdam-based roastery, located under the arch of the former Hofplein Railway viaduct, offers exceptional flat whites and top-tier beans. Renowned for its 'Vampier' blend from a Colombian coffee plantation in a region inhabited by vampire bats, Man Met Bril Koffie has become a beloved institution. The café also serves breakfast, lunch, and pastries, making it a must-visit for coffee enthusiasts in Rotterdam.

Other great places in Rotterdam are UEB West, Hopper Coffee, and Mr. Beans.

- Lola's Bikes and Coffee—The Hague:

Lola's in The Hague combines coffee with guided bike tours, creating a unique hybrid business. While enjoying some of the city's best coffee, like the rich Kampala Gold blend, you can also embark on a 'Fatbike Experience' to explore the surroundings. Lola's quirky atmosphere and commitment to supporting a cycling club in Uganda through coffee sales add to its distinctive charm.

Andere grote plaatsen in The Hague are Brood & Koffie bij Clarence, Pim Coffee Sandwiches & Vintage, en Kleine Koffiebranderij.

- Chummy Coffee, Leiden:

Housed in a former classical music shop, Chummy Coffee is one of Leiden's newest cafés.

Proprietor Jaap van der Schee, influenced by Caffeination's founder, serves exceptional coffee with a focus on quality. The café offers a variety of drinks, from straight-up filtered coffee to elaborate iced frappes and lattes featuring diverse flavors and spices. Other great places in Leiden are Borgman & Borgman, Van de Leur, Francobolli, and 't Suppiershuysinghe.

- Miss Morrison, Delft:

This small roastery in Delft, known as Miss Morrison, embraces mystery with playful responses to inquiries about its enigmatic namesake. Focused on selling freshly roasted beans for home use, Miss Morrison provides a limited menu of coffee drinks. The café's emphasis on great coffee and teas, accompanied by sweets from renowned chocolatiers, contributes to its distinct identity. These cafés offer not only exceptional coffee but also unique atmospheres, making them standouts in the vibrant Dutch coffee culture.

Dutch Coffee Gems: Beyond Delft and Groningen

- Delft:

The Buitenleven Cafe is a cozy spot in Delft, perfect for coffee lovers seeking a laid-back atmosphere and quality brews.

Uit De Kunst: A blend of art and coffee, Uit De Kunst offers a cultural experience along with your favorite cup of joe.

Kek: Known for its stylish decor and delectable coffee, Kek is a must-visit for those exploring Delft's coffee scene.

- Groningen:

Black & Bloom: Founded by coffee specialist Gerben Engelkes, Black & Bloom is the go-to spot for artisanal espresso in Groningen. With a focus on fresh, high-quality beans, it offers a tasting menu and a variety of specialty coffee drinks. **Note:** Bring a book or enjoy the moment; laptops are discouraged.

Other great places in Groningen are Masmas Groningen, Barista, and Staatse Koffiebranderij.

These additions further enrich the diverse coffee culture across the Netherlands, providing unique experiences for coffee enthusiasts in Delft and Groningen.

3.Biking Adventure

Cycling Escapades in the Netherlands

- Amsterdam City Cycling:

Explore Amsterdam's enchanting canals and historic districts on a delightful cycling tour, immersing yourself in the city's iconic charm.

Hoge Veluwe National Park Trails:

Embark on thrilling biking trails in Hoge Veluwe National Park, traversing diverse terrains from lush forests to expansive sand dunes.

- Kinderdijk Windmills Cycling Route:

Pedal through the scenic Kinderdijk countryside, marveling at UNESCO-listed windmills standing proudly along waterways.

Giethoorn Countryside Ride:

Cycle through the serene village of Giethoorn, often called the "Venice of the North," exploring its peaceful canals and thatched-roof homes.

- Texel Island Coastal Cycling:

Enjoy a coastal cycling adventure on Texel Island, discovering sandy beaches, picturesque dunes, and charming villages.

- Utrechtse Heuvelrug Forest Trails:

Delve into Utrechtse Heuvelrug National Park's forested hills and heathlands, treating yourself to panoramic views along the way.

- Limburg's Hills and Vineyards:

Conquer the hills of Limburg, cycling through scenic vineyards, traditional villages, and the picturesque Maas River valley.

- Zuiderzee Cycling Route:

Embark on the Zuiderzee Cycling Route, encircling the former Zuiderzee and exploring historic towns like Enkhuizen en Hoorn.

- Groningen City and Countryside Ride:

Bike through Groningen's cityscape, then venture into the tranquil countryside, passing farms and expansive landscapes.

- Amstel River Cycle Path:

Follow the Amstel River Cycle Path, winding through the Dutch countryside, passing by historic castles and picturesque estates.

- Drentsche Aa National Landscape Ride:

Explore the protected Drentsche Aa National Landscape, cycling through charming villages, meandering streams, and ancient burial mounds.

- Zeeland's Coastal Dike Cycling:

Cycle along Zeeland's coastal dikes, savoring panoramic views of the North Sea and discovering delightful coastal towns.

The Netherlands' diverse biking adventures promise a fusion of natural beauty, cultural exploration, and outdoor excitement, catering to cyclists of all skill levels. Get ready to pedal through a cyclist's paradise!

Chapter Three

Dutch Adventures

A.Cycling Expeditions

Holland is renowned as a cycling country, with 17 million inhabitants owning bikes. The extensive cycling infrastructure includes 33,000 km of cycle paths, cycle routes, bridges, tunnels, ferries, and special signposts. Cycling is ingrained in daily life, with parents taking children to school, workers commuting, and even the prime minister using a bike. Given the Netherlands' watery landscape, exploring the country from both the saddle and the water is a logical choice.

Cycletours Holidays introduced bike and barge tours in 1987, offering a unique way to experience the Netherlands. The country's flat terrain ensures a mountain-free cycling tour. Special tulip tours between April and mid-May focus on the tulip theme, including a visit to the iconic Keukenhof. The tulip, originating in Turkey, reached the Netherlands in the late 16th century, leading to a flourishing trade. The tulip tour takes cyclists through vast tulip fields, and entry to Keukenhof is included.

- Amsterdam:

Founded in the 12th century, Amsterdam started as a small settlement at the mouth of the river Amstel. The construction of a dam in Amstel marked its beginning. Over the centuries, Amsterdam expanded, and in the 17th and 18th centuries, it became one of the most prosperous European cities. The famous canals were dug during the Golden Age, with merchants building ornate mansions.

Amsterdam offers a wealth of attractions, including the canals, the Jordaan area, Vondelpark, Leidseplein, Rembrandtplein, the Spiegel district's antique shops, and Museum Square with the Rijksmuseum, Stedelijk Museum, Van Gogh Museum, and the Anne Frank House.

- Bike and Barge Tours:

Bike & Barge holidays provide a unique experience, combining cycling with a floating hotel. The floating hotel sails to the next stage while cyclists pedal along. Participants enjoy a pleasant atmosphere on board, socialize, and have specially prepared meals. Evening relaxation includes drinks in the salon or enjoying the sunset on deck.

Tours start and/or finish in the city center of Amsterdam, with various routes available. Popular options include Amsterdam to Bruges or Koblenz. Classic tours in Holland cover Texel, Haarlem, Leiden, Delft, Kinderdijk, and Gouda. The Rhine and IJssel tour explores the eastern part of the country, while the Friesland and Lake IJssel tour delves into villages from the Golden Age and the rural province of Friesland.

For more information or assistance, the Cycletours Holidays office in Amsterdam is available to provide advice and answer questions. Cycling in the Netherlands is a daily affair for locals but offers a new and exciting experience for visitors.

B. Windmill Tours and Historic Sites

The Dutch landscape is synonymous with windmills, making them a must-see when visiting the Netherlands. Here's a guide to the best places to experience these iconic structures:

Fun Facts about Dutch Windmills:

The oldest existing windmill in the Netherlands is the Grafelijke Korenmolen in Zeddam, built around 1440.

The oldest historical record of windmills in the Netherlands dates back to 1221, mentioning the windmill in Willemskerke, a village that no longer exists.

The windmills of Schiedam, once numbering about 20, are the tallest in the world. The tallest non-historical windmill is De Nolet (42.5

m), built in 2005, and the tallest historical windmill is De Noord (33.3 m).

The Best Places to See Windmills:

- Kinderdijk Windmills:

Located at a UNESCO World Heritage Site, Kinderdijk boasts 19 windmills, showcasing the largest concentration in the Netherlands. Originally built to drain water from polders, these windmills offer a picturesque view.

- Zaanse Schans Windmill Village:

Zaanse Schans, near Amsterdam, is renowned for its historic windmills (15 in total) and traditional Dutch life. Visitors can witness the workings of various mills, from grinding to sawing.

- De Schermer Windmills:

De Schermer features 11 windmills that played a crucial role in draining water from the polders, reclaiming land for use. The windmills add to the scenic beauty of the landscape.

- De Adriaan in Haarlem:

De Adriaan, located in Haarlem, stands as a symbol of the city and offers panoramic views.

Although rebuilt over time, it remains an iconic structure in Haarlem.

- The Keukenhof Windmill:

Situated in Keukenhof, famous for its tulip fields, this windmill adds charm to the vibrant flower landscape.

Visitors can enjoy the beauty of tulips in full bloom.

- Windmills in Heusden:

Heusden features charming windmills that enhance the town's historical ambiance.

These windmills contribute to the overall character of the fortified town.

- Windmills in Wemeldinge:

Wemeldinge boasts beautiful windmills, enhancing the scenic allure of the region.

These windmills showcase the historical significance of wind power in the Netherlands.

- Windmills in Amsterdam:

While not the most prominent feature in Amsterdam, several windmills, including De Gooyer, De Otter, and The Mill of Sloten, add historical charm to the city.

Best Windmill Tours from Amsterdam:
Various tours offer experiences at famous windmill sites like Kinderdijk and Zaanse Schans.

- Final Words:

Celebrate National Windmill Day every second weekend in May, when many windmills, typically closed to the public, open their doors for visitors.

When exploring the Netherlands, a visit to at least one of these windmill-rich locations ensures an authentic experience, connecting you to the country's rich history and picturesque landscapes.

- The Kinderdijk Windmills:

Kinderdijk, about 1 hour and 15 minutes from Amsterdam, is renowned for its 19 windmills and remarkable water-management system.

A UNESCO World Heritage Site, these 18th-century windmills were vital for pumping water out of the once-boggy landscape.

- Zaanse Schans Windmill Village:

Located just 20 km from Amsterdam, Zaanse Schans is an open-air museum village offering insights into 18th and 19th-century Dutch life. Established in the 1960s–70s, the village features historic buildings and windmills transported from the Zaan area.

- De Schermer Windmills:

The 11 polder windmills in Schermer played a key role in reclaiming land from water in a major Dutch land reclamation project. The Museum Mill in Schermerhorn is part of a complex of three polder windmills, showcasing their impressive water-pumping capabilities.

- De Adriaan in Haarlem:

De Adriaan, a symbol of Haarlem, was built in 1778 and used for cement production from tuff stone.

After being destroyed by fire in 1932, it was painstakingly restored and reopened as a museum in 2002.

- The Keukenhof Windmill:

In Keukenhof, the world's largest tulip garden, a charming windmill offers panoramic views of tulip fields and the park.

While not the main attraction, the windmill complements the stunning tulip displays.

- The Windmills in Heusden:

Heusden, a well-preserved fortified town in North Brabant, showcases windmills that enhance its historical ambiance.

Restored to a 1649 map, Heusden provides a glimpse into Dutch life from centuries ago.

- The windmills in Wemeldinge:

Wemeldinge features beautiful windmills, adding to the scenic allure of the region.

These windmills contribute to the historical significance of wind power in the Netherlands.

Where to see windmills in Amsterdam:

Amsterdam may not be known for its windmills, but there are notable ones, including De Gooyer, De Otter, The Mill of Sloten, De Riekermolen, and d'Admiraal.

The Best Windmill Tours from Amsterdam:

Various tours offer experiences at famous windmill sites like Kinderdijk and Zaanse Schans.

Final Words:

Celebrate National Windmill Day every second weekend in May, when many windmills are open to the public.

Whether it's the iconic Kinderdijk or the historical charm of Heusden, exploring these windmill-rich locations provides a unique glimpse into Dutch culture and engineering prowess.

When visiting the Netherlands, immerse yourself in the beauty of these windmills, each with its own story and contribution to the country's rich heritage.

Where to see windmills in the Netherlands?

- Kinderdijk Windmills:

Location: Near Rotterdam

Remarkable for its 19 windmills built in the 18th century, showcasing Dutch water-management expertise.

Recognized as a UNESCO World Heritage Site.

Ideal day trip from Amsterdam, approximately 1 hour and 15 minutes away.

- Zaanse Schans Windmill Village:

Location: 20 km from Amsterdam

A charming open-air museum village reflecting life in the 18th and 19th centuries.

Created in the 1960s-70s, featuring historical buildings and windmills transported from various areas.

Zaanse Schans Card offers access to multiple attractions.

- De Schermer Windmills:

Location: Schermerhorn, 40 km from Amsterdam

11 remaining polder windmills integral to a significant land reclamation project.

The Museum Mill in Schermerhorn showcases the water-pumping capabilities of these historic mills.

- De Adriaan in Haarlem:

Location: Haarlem

A famous windmill integral to the cityscape, initially built in 1778 for cement production.

Destroyed in 1932, meticulously restored and reopened in 2002 as a museum.

An iconic symbol of Haarlem.

- The Keukenhof Windmill:

Location: Keukenhof Gardens

Offers a picturesque view of tulip fields and the park.

A lovely addition to the world's largest tulip garden.

- Windmills in Heusden:

Location: North Brabant, near Den Bosch

Restored town reflecting the 17th-century landscape, with three windmills added in the 1970s.

A fortified town with a historic charm.

- Windmills in Wemeldinge:

Location: Zeeland

Houses two windmills, De Hoop (1866) and Aeolus (1869), showcasing historical grain milling.

De Hoop was restored in the 1980s, and Aeolus can be visited monthly.

Tip: National Windmill Day is celebrated every 2nd weekend in May, providing public access to numerous windmills that are usually closed.

Explore the Dutch countryside and witness the engineering marvels that have shaped the landscape throughout history.

Chapternsive sandy shores, complemented by beachside cafes and the iconic Pier.

- Zandvoort aan Zee, North Holland:

Experience the lively atmosphere, wide sandy stretches, and water sports at Zandvoort's vibrant beach.

- Texel Island Seaside Escapes:

Discover serene Texel Island beaches surrounded by dunes, offering tranquility and beachcombing opportunities.

- Egmond aan Zee, North Holland:

Enjoy family-friendly Egmond aan Zee beach, exploring lighthouses and trying various beach activities.

- Domburg, Zeeland:

Unwind on Domburg's charming beaches, known for cleanliness and historic seaside architecture.

- Noordwijk Beach, South Holland:

Relax on the clean, well-facilitated beaches of Noordwijk, accompanied by beachside cafes and restaurants.

- Ameland Island Coastal Retreats:

Experience natural beauty on Ameland's beaches, surrounded by dunes and offering a peaceful retreat.

- Cadzand Beach, Zeeland:
Visit Cadzand for wide, clean beaches and explore nearby nature reserves amidst stunning coastal scenery.
- Katwijk aan Zee, South Holland:
Explore family-friendly Katwijk aan Zee beach, known for its relaxed atmosphere and historic lighthouse.
- Vlieland Island Relaxation:
Escape to Vlieland's tranquil beaches, surrounded by nature reserves, for a serene coastal retreat.
- Dutch Wadden Islands Adventures:
Discover unique beaches on the Wadden Islands, each offering its own character, from lively to secluded.
- Holland's Coastal Cycling Routes:
Explore coastal areas by bike using dedicated cycling routes, uncovering hidden beaches and breathtaking sea views.

Whether you seek peaceful retreats or exciting beach activities, the Netherlands' diverse coastline has the perfect coastal escape for every preference.

D. Water sports in Zeeland

- Diverse Water Adventures:

In Zeeland, discover beaches with ideal winds for various water sports, from calm Veerse Meer Lake to thrilling open North Sea spots.

- Water Sports Extravaganza:

Zeeland caters to water sports fanatics, offering a plethora of activities like kitesurfing, wave surfing, waterskiing, wakeboarding, blokarting, paddleboarding, kayaking, and more.

- Snorkeling and diving:

Dive into the underwater wonders with snorkeling or diving options. Choose your aquatic adventure from this extensive menu of water sports.

- Surfing Bliss:

Embrace the thrill of surfing in Zeeland's serial waves and cool beaches. Whether you're a seasoned surfer or a novice, Zeeland's coast has the perfect spot for everyone.

- Windsurfing Wonderland:

Explore the colorful world of windsurfing at Het Veerse Meer and Grevelingen. Lessons are available for all ages, teaching not only windsurfing techniques but also how to read the wind.

- Conquer the waves:

Challenge the great waves of the North Sea with wave surfing in Domburg, one of the top hotspots in the country. Enjoy the clear waters and sandy beaches, making it an ideal surfing retreat.

- Kitesurfing Adventure:

Zeeland offers astounding beaches for kitesurfing, including Brouwersdam, Neeltje Jans, Kamperland, Vrouwenpolder, Domburg, and Cadzand. Experience the thrill of being yanked up over the water by the wind.

- Brouwersdam Haven:

Brouwersdam stands out as Zeeland's most popular water sport haven, offering wind most of the time, making it ideal for windsurfing, kitesurfing, wave surfing, and blokarting. It's a cool launch spot for surfing careers.

- Gear Rental and Lessons:

Surfing shops and schools abound in Zeeland, providing gear for rent or purchase. Whether you're a beginner or a seasoned surfer, lessons are available to enhance your skills and enjoyment.

Experience the ultimate water sports adventure in Zeeland, where the wind is right, the waves are thrilling, and the possibilities are endless.

Chapter Four

Cultural Immersion

A. Dutch cuisine and culinary delights

While the Netherlands may not have gained international fame as a culinary destination, its cuisine offers a delightful mix of snacks, desserts, seafood, and cheeses. Despite a historical lack of exotic spices in traditional dishes, Dutch cuisine has evolved to embrace influences from various cultures, including Jewish, Turkish, Indonesian, and Surinamese.

- Historical Roots:

Dutch cuisine has historical roots depicted in art, such as Vincent van Gogh's "The Potato Eaters," reflecting a time when potatoes, bread, and porridge were staple foods. The Golden Age brought prosperity, introducing spices, sugar, and exotic fruits. Wealthier households enjoyed international flavors, leading to the tradition of spiced cookies like speculaas.

- 20th Century and Beyond:

In the 20th century, Dutch women learned cooking skills in schools focused on domestic work, promoting simplicity, frugality, and nutrition. This commitment to healthy eating continues today, with the Netherlands earning recognition for having a plentiful, affordable, and nutritious diet.

- Influences of Colonization and Immigration:

Colonization, as seen in the Dutch rule over Indonesia, contributed to Dutch-Indonesian fusion recipes becoming national dishes. Suriname, another former Dutch colony, also enriched Dutch cuisine with unique flavors.

- Dutch Diet Today:

A 2016 report by the Rijksinstituut voor Volksgezondheid en Milieu (RIVM) revealed that the Dutch have a diverse diet, with high consumption of beverages, dairy, snacks, desserts, sugar, and fats. The Dutch typically eat six or seven times a day, with an emphasis on home-cooked meals and family dinners.

- Flexitarian and Sustainable Trends: Approximately one in three people in the Netherlands identifies as a flexitarian, choosing not to eat meat daily. Vegetarianism, veganism, and sustainable food movements are gaining popularity, especially in Dutch cities.

In conclusion, while Dutch cuisine may have humble historical beginnings, it has evolved into a diverse and dynamic culinary landscape, shaped by historical influences and contemporary trends. Whether savoring traditional favorites or exploring modern twists, the Netherlands has a unique culinary identity waiting to be discovered.

- Breakfast in the Netherlands:

Breakfast, known as "ontbijt," doesn't receive much attention, with many Dutch people skipping it. When they do have breakfast, it often includes high-starch and high-sugar items. A quirky trend is the consumption of "hagelslag," chocolate sprinkles on buttered bread.

- Lunch in the Netherlands:

Lunch is a social affair in the Netherlands, with workers taking breaks together. It typically consists of simple sandwiches ("boterham") with butter, ham, or cheese. This meal emphasizes workplace bonding and socializing.

- Dinner in the Netherlands:

Dutch dinners are eaten relatively early, around 18:00, and are usually enjoyed at home with family. A favorite dish is "stamppot," mashed potatoes with vegetables, served with smoked sausage and gravy.

- Snacks in the Netherlands:

The Dutch enjoy "borrel" in the late afternoon or early evening, a time for socializing, having local beers and wine, and indulging in fried snacks. "Bitterballen," hot fried balls of meat or mushroom ragout, are a popular choice during this time.

- Special meals in the Netherlands:

Christmas Meal:

Families celebrate either on December 25 or 26, enjoying "kerststol" for brunch and feasting on dishes like "rollade" or roasted meats for dinner. "Gourmetten" is a popular cozy way of sharing a meal during Christmas.

New Year's Eve Meal:

The New Year is welcomed with "oliebollen," deep-fried dough balls, and other treats like "appelbeignets" (apple fritters) and "ananas beignets" (pineapple fritters).

Easter Meal:

Easter Sunday is celebrated with brunch and egg hunts. Common foods include rolls, cheese, ham, eggs, and "paasbrood" (spiced bread with raisins and dried fruit).

Birthday Meal:

Dutch birthday traditions involve bringing a cake to share with colleagues. Traditional birthday celebrations include sitting in a circle, enjoying coffee, and "appeltaart" (apple pie).

Popular Ingredients:

Dutch cuisine often features dishes with meat, starch, and vegetables. Seafood is prevalent in coastal provinces like Zeeland. Common ingredients include potatoes, vegetables, cheese, and various meats.

In summary, Dutch eating habits are marked by simplicity, socialization during meals, and a blend of traditional and modern culinary trends. From everyday meals to festive occasions, Dutch cuisine reflects a unique cultural identity.

Meats in the Netherlands:

The Dutch have substantial meat consumption, with an average person eating over 77 kg of meat annually. Pork (varkensvlees) is a major part of Dutch cuisine, used in the popular smoked sausage known as "rookworst." Diced pork belly, or spek, is a key ingredient in dishes like erwtensoep (pea soup). Beef (rundvlees) is also widely consumed, with cuts like stoofvlees (stew meat), biefstuk (steak), kogelbiefstuk (rump steak), and haasbiefstuk (tenderloin) being popular. Hachée, a slow-cooked beef stew with caramelized onions, is a winter favorite.

Chicken (kip) is another significant meat, with kipsaté being a popular dish. This Indonesian-influenced dish consists of grilled chicken skewers covered in sataysaus (satay sauce) and served with french fries.

Fish in the Netherlands:

Given its maritime history, seafood holds a special place in Dutch cuisine. Common locally sourced fish include plaice (schol), herring (haring), mackerel (makreel), cod (kabeljauw), haddock (schelvis), mussels (mosselen), and eel (paling). Salted raw herring (Hollandse nieuwe haring) is a Dutch delicacy, enjoyed traditionally between May and July. Flag Day (Vlaggetjesdag) is a festival dedicated to herring, celebrating the return of the herring fleet.

Vegetables in the Netherlands:

The Netherlands is a top vegetable grower and exporter, ensuring fresh vegetables year-round. Root and cruciferous vegetables are prevalent, including potatoes (aardappelen), carrots (wortels), kale (boerenkool), white asparagus (Witte or Brabantse Wal asperges), parsnip (pastinaak), endive (andijvie), leek (prei), beets (bieten), spinach (spinazie), chicory (witlof), and Brussels sprouts (spruitjes).

Carbohydrates in the Netherlands:

Bread (brood) is a staple in the Dutch diet, often consumed with every meal. Alongside sandwich bread, specialty bread includes krentenbollen (sweet bread rolls with currants and raisins), roggebrood (dark, dense rye bread, often eaten with spek), and ontbijtkoek (spiced rye cake).

B. Traditional Festivals and Celebrations

- January:

New Year's Day Dive (Nieuwjaarsduik):
Take a chilly dive into the North Sea, followed by erwtensoep (pea soup) to warm up.
Rotterdam International Film Festival:
Enjoy quality independent films from around the world in Rotterdam.

- February:

Lunar New Year:
Celebrate Chinese New Year with dragon parades, lion dances, and delicious Chinese cuisine.

- March:

Carnival (Mardi Gras), Maastricht:
Join one of Europe's biggest and most lively carnivals in Maastricht.

- April:

King's Day (Koningsdag), Amsterdam: Experience a massive street party, flea markets, and lively celebrations in honor of King Willem-Alexander.

World Press Photo Exhibition: Witness powerful photojournalism in this global exhibition.

- May:

Flower Parade (Bloemencorso), Noordwijk to Haarlem: Marvel at a colorful procession of flower floats from Noordwijk to Haarlem.

Amsterdam Gay Pride: Enjoy the Canal Parade, street discos, and open-air theater performances during this LGBTQ+ celebration.

- June:

Rotterdam Summer Carnival (Zomercarnaval): Experience Latin music and Brazilian energy in Rotterdam.

North Sea Jazz Festival, Rotterdam:

Immerse yourself in world-class jazz performances.

- July:

Scheveningen International Fireworks Festival (Vuurwerkfestival):
Witness a spectacular fireworks competition on the Scheveningen beach.

Amsterdam Gay Pride:
Continue the festivities, including the Canal Parade and cultural events.

- August:

Amsterdam Canal Festival (Grachtenfestival):
Enjoy classical music in unique architectural venues.

Jordaan Festival, Amsterdam:
Experience diverse Dutch music genres in the trendy Jordaan neighborhood.

- September:

There were no notable events.

- October:

Relief of Leiden (Leidens Ontzet):
Commemorate the lifting of the Spanish siege with processions, festivities, and traditional Dutch treats.

- November:

St. Nicholas (Sinterklaas), Amsterdam:
Witness the largest Saint Nicholas parade in the world, featuring Sinterklaas and his Zwarte Pieten.

- December:

Christmas:
Celebrate Christmas on December 25th and 26th with traditional festivities and store closures.

Embark on a year-round journey through the Netherlands, where culinary delights and festive celebrations showcase the rich tapestry of Dutch culture.

C. Arts and Architecture

Art

Jacob van Ruysdael (1628–82): Renowned for his landscape mastery, Van Ruysdael captured the essence of Dutch life in cornfields, windmills, and forest scenes. His expansive skies, filled with moody clouds, adorn canvases that celebrate the flat Dutch terrain.

Frans Hals (1581-1666): Leading the Haarlem school, Hals excelled in portraiture, revolutionizing the genre with relaxed subjects and light brushstrokes. The Frans Hals Museum in Haarlem provides insight into his groundbreaking techniques.

Rembrandt van Rijn (1606–69): A luminary of Western art, Rembrandt's work delved into the soul and inner life of humanity. The Night Watch (1642), housed in the Rijksmuseum, stands as a testament to his mastery. His self-portraits, reflecting his life's journey, are poignant displays of spirituality.

Jan Vermeer (1632–75): Known for focusing on home life, Vermeer's paintings exude simplicity and serenity. Placing figures at the center, he skillfully used backgrounds to convey stability. His work illuminates the pleasures of everyday activities.

Vincent van Gogh (1853–90): Van Gogh's journey from a failed missionary to a revered artist unfolded with masterpieces like The Potato Eaters (1885). His later works, inspired by the Mediterranean sun, showcased vibrant colors, notably his beloved yellow. The Van Gogh Museum in Amsterdam houses a rich collection of over 200 paintings.

Piet Mondrian (1872–1944): Before pioneering De Stijl, Mondrian painted windmills and meadows. The Red Tree (1909) marked a shift towards neoplasticism, emphasizing purified abstraction. His journey mirrored an evolution from Impressionism to a revolutionary artistic movement.

Architecture

Strap and Scroll Ornament (16th–17th centuries): The strap and scroll ornament, resembling curled leather, gained popularity during this period. Step gables, resembling small staircases, adorned many canal-side buildings. Hendrick de Keyser, an architect in Amsterdam, creatively blended decorative elements like volutes and masks with practical materials, creating visually dynamic facades.

Renaissance and Ornate Step Gables: Architects like Philips and Justus Vingboons ushered in an era where medieval step gables evolved into more ornate versions. The addition of scrolled sides, decorative finials, and other Renaissance features transformed the cityscape along Herengracht, Keizersgracht, and Prinsengracht.

Classical Period (17th century): Jacob van Campen, renowned for the Town Hall (now Royal Palace), played a pivotal role in the classical period. The shift to classical elements led to more boxed-in, central facades with straight lines, departing from the flowing Renaissance style.

Adriaan Dortsman (1665): Dortsman introduced a restrained Dutch style around 1665, featuring homes with balconies and attics. His designs omitted the pilasters and festoons prevalent in earlier facades.

Amsterdam School (1900–1940): A diverse range of architectural styles emerged during this period, but the Amsterdam School architects stood out. They crafted brickwork that transcended earlier fantasies, creating massive yet fluid buildings adorned with stained glass, wrought iron, and distinctive corner towers.

Chapter Five

Local Experiences

A.Cheese tasting in Gouda

- Gouda Cheese Market:

Begin your journey at the iconic Gouda Cheese Market, hosted in the town's historic market square.

- Historic Cheese Weighing House:

Experience traditional cheese weighing ceremonies at the historic Cheese Weighing House in Gouda.

- Cheese shops in Gouda:

Wander through charming Gouda streets, adorned with cheese shops offering a diverse array of Gouda cheese wheels, both young and aged.

- Cheese Museums:

Dive into the history and production of Gouda cheese at the Cheese and Crafts Museum or the Gouda Cheese Experience.

- Farm Visits:

Embark on a journey to local farms surrounding Gouda for an authentic farm-to-table cheese tasting experience.

- Cheese Workshops:

Gain hands-on experience in crafting Gouda cheese by participating in a cheese-making workshop.

- Cheese Pairing Events:

Attend cheese pairing events in Gouda, where experts guide you through the art of pairing Gouda with wine, beer, and local accompaniments.

- Gouda Cheese Museum:

Immerse yourself in the Gouda cheese world at the Gouda Cheese Museum, featuring exhibits and tastings.

- Cheese Tasting Tours:

Join guided cheese tasting tours in Gouda, where experts introduce you to the nuances of different Gouda cheese varieties.

- Cheese Markets Beyond Gouda:

Explore nearby cheese markets in Woerden, Alkmaar, or Edam, each offering a unique cheese-tasting experience.

- Cheese and Wine Cruises:

Combine a scenic canal cruise with cheese and wine tasting, allowing you to savor Gouda in a picturesque setting.

- Gouda Cheese Trails:

Follow dedicated cheese trails in and around Gouda, discovering local cheese producers and enjoying tastings along the way.

Indulge in the rich and creamy flavors of Gouda cheese, where traditions and innovations merge to create a delightful tasting experience.

B. Kinderdijk Windmills

The Kinderdijk windmills, comprising 19 monumental structures, stand proudly in the Alblasserwaard polder, South Holland. Built in 1738 and 1740, these mills, primarily in Kinderdijk village, combat water issues in the polder, forming the largest concentration of historic windmills in the Netherlands. Notable for their preservation, they've been a UNESCO World Heritage Site since 1997, known officially as the Mill Network at Kinderdijk-Elshout.

Situated at the confluence of the Lek and Noord rivers, Kinderdijk addresses water problems dating back to the 13th century. Extensive canals were initially dug, but with soil settling and river levels rising, windmills emerged as a vital solution around 1738. While some still operate, diesel pumping stations now handle the primary water management, showcasing the Dutch ingenuity in hydraulic engineering.

C. Delft Pottery Workshops

Embark on a pottery adventure starting at the Royal Delft Factory, the sole surviving Delftware factory from the 17th century. Delve into the artistry and history of Delftware with guided tours and workshops, where skilled artisans share traditional techniques, including hand-painting and glazing.

Explore the Delft Pottery Museum to deepen your understanding before immersing yourself in Delft Blue painting classes. Enroll in workshops across local pottery studios, offering hands-on experiences. Engage in Delftware tile workshops, crafting decorative tiles with timeless designs.

Combine pottery sessions with city tours, discovering Delft's historic sites and artistic heritage. Family-friendly options cater to all ages, allowing everyone to create Delftware treasures. Keep an eye out for seasonal events, adding a festive touch to your creative journey. Customize your pottery creations, adding a personal touch, and consider Delftware masterclasses for advanced insights. Craft your own Delft pottery souvenirs, creating lasting memories of your artistic exploration in Delft. Immerse yourself in the world of Delft pottery, where learning, creating, and appreciating converge in a timeless experience.

Chapter Six

Practical Tips

A. Language and local etiquette

Welcome to the vibrant world of Dutch culture, where the Dutch language thrives as a fascinating West Germanic gem. Spoken by over 25 million as a first language and 5 million as a second language, Dutch takes its place as the third most widely spoken Germanic language, right after its close cousins English and German.

In South Africa and Namibia, Afrikaans, a sister language to Dutch, flourishes as a derivative of earlier Dutch forms, creating a linguistic bridge for at least 16 million speakers. Across Belgium, including Flemish and Suriname, Dutch holds sway, guided by the Dutch Language Union.

In Europe, Dutch resonates through the Netherlands and 60% of Belgium's population, while Suriname and the Caribbean islands of Aruba, Curaçao, and Sint Maarten proudly claim it as their own. Not to be forgotten are the linguistic echoes in the United States, Canada, and Australia, where half a million native speakers reside.

Dutch, a linguistic cousin to both German and English, stands unique, avoiding the High German consonant shift and the use of Germanic umlaut. Its rich vocabulary, predominantly Germanic with a hint of Romance, captivates the linguistic explorer.

Navigating Dutch Etiquette

Basic Etiquette:

- As you traverse the Dutch social landscape, remember these key points:

Greet with a wave and a friendly "Goedemorgen" or "Goedemiddag."

Punctuality is golden; always warn if tardiness is imminent.

Cover your mouth when yawning, and avoid speaking while chewing gum.

Knock before entering a closed room, and keep hands out of pockets.

Save compliments for private conversations.

Phone calls begin with stating names with a courteous touch.

Acknowledge a sneeze with a hearty "gezondheid" (bless you).

- Visiting:

Unlock the door to Dutch hospitality.

Plan visits in advance; unexpected visits are rare.

Coffee dates in public spaces are preferred over home invitations.

Timeliness matters; arrive promptly.

Greet everyone, including children, upon arrival.

A small gift for the host is customary; avoid requesting home tours.

Social visits shine, especially during birthdays.

Parties may stretch late into the night; be prepared to linger.

- Eating:

Delight in Dutch dining traditions:

Dinner reigns supreme, commencing around 6 p.m.

Wait for the host's cue to begin eating.

"Eet Smakelijk" signals the start; keep hands above the table until the meal ends.

Opt for modest portions; finishing your plate is appreciated.

Bills are often split equally among couples, while groups pay individually.

Gifts:

Mastering the art of gifting in Dutch culture:

Bring chocolates, flowers, or a book when visiting.

Avoid white lilies or chrysanthemums; they symbolize mourning.

Gifts are opened in the giver's presence.

Choose thoughtful gestures over extravagant gifts to ensure comfort.

B.Safety Guidelines

- COVID-19 Precautions:

Stay informed on the latest COVID-19 guidelines from Dutch health authorities. Maintain proper hygiene by using hand sanitizers and washing your hands frequently.

- Emergency Services:

Know the emergency contact number, 112, for police, fire, and medical emergencies.

- Travel Insurance:

Consider travel insurance that covers medical emergencies and unexpected events.

- Public transportation safety:

Be vigilant against pickpocketing, especially in crowded places. Adhere to safety guidelines when using trains, buses, and trams.

- Bicycle Safety:

Follow traffic rules and wear a helmet while cycling. Securely lock your bicycle when not in use.

- Water Safety:

Exercise caution around water, especially during water activities.

Follow safety instructions at beaches and lakes.

- Weather Preparedness:

Stay informed about the weather forecast, especially for outdoor activities.

Be ready for sudden weather changes.

- Healthcare Services:

Know the locations of healthcare facilities and pharmacies in your area.

Ensure access to necessary medications and be aware of the local emergency medical number.

- Traffic Safety:

When crossing the street, make sure you look both ways and use the designated crosswalks.

Follow traffic rules and signals when driving or walking.

- Cultural Sensitivity:

Respect local customs and traditions.

Familiarize yourself with and adhere to cultural etiquette specific to the region.

- Internet and Cybersecurity:

Use secure Wi-Fi connections, especially for sensitive information.

Exercise caution when sharing personal details online.

- Natural Hazards:

Stay informed about natural hazards and follow local guidance.

Know evacuation routes if you live in an area prone to natural disasters.

- Stay Updated:

Recognize that safety guidelines may change, so stay updated with reliable sources.

Always apply common sense and caution for a secure and enjoyable experience in the Netherlands.

C.Sustainable Travel Practices

- Efficient Public Transportation:

Opt for eco-friendly trains, trams, and buses to minimize your carbon footprint.

- Cycling Culture:

Embrace Dutch cycling by renting bikes for city exploration and scenic journeys.

- Electric Vehicles:

Consider electric vehicle rentals for longer trips to support sustainable transport.

- Eco-Certified Accommodations:

Choose lodgings with eco-certifications committed to practices like recycling and energy conservation.

- Local and Sustainable Cuisine:

Support regional agriculture by dining at restaurants serving local, organic, and sustainably sourced food.

- Waste Reduction:

Carry a reusable water bottle and shopping bag to minimize single-use plastic.

Dispose of waste responsibly, following local recycling guidelines.

- Nature Conservation:

Respect designated paths in nature reserves to minimize environmental impact.

- Energy-Efficient Practices:

When not in use, turn off lights and electronics in lodgings to save energy.

- Cultural Respect:

Uphold local customs, contributing to cultural preservation and responsible tourism.

- Nature-Friendly Activities:

Engage in wildlife tours, hiking, or bird watching to promote environmental awareness.

- Clean-Up Initiatives:

Join local clean-up programs to contribute to the preservation of natural landscapes.

- Educate Yourself:

Stay informed on sustainable travel practices in the Netherlands, minimizing your ecological impact.

By adopting these sustainable practices, you not only reduce your environmental impact but also play a part in preserving the natural and cultural heritage of the Netherlands.

Chapter Seven

Accommodations

A. Charming hotels and bed and breakfasts

Ambassade Hotel

- Hotel Details:
- Address: Herengracht 341, Amsterdam, North Holland, 1016 AZ, Netherlands
- Telephone: 00 31 2055 5022 2
- Bedrooms: 3 suites, 19 superior rooms, 25 classic rooms, 6 small standard rooms, and 3 family rooms.
- Facilities: lifts, lobby, 2 lounges, breakfast room, two meeting rooms, library, internet facility, library bar, Brasserie Ambassade. Free wireless internet. Float and massage centers are nearby. Bicycle hire (€17.50 daily). Unsuitable for disabled people.

- Children: Yes, family rooms and cots are available.
- Credit Cards: Amex, Master, Visa, JCB.

A Long-Time Guide Favorite:

This hotel, a long-time favorite, spans ten 17th-century gabled houses along the serene canals of Herengracht and Singel. Within walking distance of major attractions, each room, carefully restored, exudes unique character. The hotel boasts a remarkable modern art collection, with the avant-garde Cobra movement as its centerpiece. The library/bar showcases signed first editions from authors who've stayed, creating a literary haven. A unique float and massage center, "Koan Float," adds to the allure. Enjoy the lavish breakfast in the French-style Brasserie Ambassade.

Canal House Hotel:

- Address: Keizersgracht 148, Amsterdam, North Holland, 1015 CX, Netherlands
- Telephone: 00 31 2062 2518 2
- Bedrooms: 23 rooms.
- Facilities: air conditioning, Wi-Fi, garden, terrace, bar, room service, concierge.
- Background music: yes.
- Children: Yes.
- Dogs: No.
- Credit Cards: All major cards are accepted.

Glamorous Contemporary Gem:

Nestled in a 17th-century house in the Bohemian Jordaan district, this glamorous hotel, under new ownership, reopened in 2010 after an extensive renovation. Retaining its historic charm, the hotel offers contemporary comfort. Rooms, adorned in dark purple hues, provide a cozy retreat. The Great Room, serving breakfast until late, overlooks a garden, offering a serene start to your day. Hostaria, an excellent Italian restaurant, awaits nearby.

Hotel de l'Europe:

- Address: Nieuwe Doelenstraat 2-14, Amsterdam, North Holland, 1012 CP, Netherlands
- Telephone: 00 31 253 1177 7
- Bedrooms: 111 rooms.
- Facilities: lift, air-conditioning, room service, bar, restaurants, Wi-Fi, parking, concierge, spa, fitness center with pool, terrace, bicycle rental.
- Background music: yes.
- Children: Yes.
- Dogs: Yes.
- Credit Cards: All major cards are accepted.

Historic Grandeur on the Canals:

Situated at the junction of the River Amstel and canals, this 19th-century beauty combines grandeur with family warmth. Indulge in the collection of Dutch landscapes and fine dining at Bord'Eau, helmed by Gault Millau Chef of the Year 2014. The fitness center offers a Grecian-style pool. Immerse yourself in the rich surroundings, with Rembrandt's house and the Rijksmuseum nearby.

Hotel Toren:

- Address: Keizersgracht 164, Amsterdam, North Holland, 1015 CZ, Netherlands
- Telephone: 00 31 2062 2635 2
- Bedrooms: 38 rooms.
- Facilities: air conditioning, Wi-Fi, lift, restaurant, bar.
- Background music: Yes, in the bar.
- Children: Yes.
- Dogs: Yes, for a small supplement.
- Credit Cards: All major cards are accepted.

Opulent Elegance by the Canal:

Under the ownership of Eric and Petra Toren, this opulent hotel offers excellent customer service in two 17th-century canal houses. Individually decorated rooms range from compact to spacious, creating a warm and romantic ambiance. The hotel bar doubles as a charming breakfast spot, offering a delightful start to your day.

Hotel V Nesplein:

- Address: Nes 49, Amsterdam, North Holland, 1012 KD, Netherlands
- Telephone: 00 31 2066 2323 3
- Bedrooms: 43 rooms.
- Facilities: restaurant/bar/lounge, air conditioning, Wi-Fi, room service, lift, concierge.
- Children: Yes, cots and extra beds are available.
- Dogs: No.
- Credit Cards: All major cards are accepted.

Urban Chic in the Theatre District:

In the heart of the theater district, Hotel V Nesplein offers ultra-stylish rooms with an industrial, loft-style vibe. Owned by a family, this hotel, opened in 2013, features a vibrant lobby with a restaurant, bar, and terrace. Rooms simply furnished with vintage pieces create a trendy yet cozy atmosphere. Explore

Dam Square and the Anne Frank House, just a short walk away.

B.Houseboats and Unique Stays

- Luxury Houseboat in Maastricht:

Located in a picturesque marina surrounded by the South Limburg Hills,.

Spacious 12x4-meter houseboat with 2 bedrooms and queen-size beds.

Stunning views, close to Maastricht, Geul, and Gulp valleys.

Bathroom with shower and toilet; can accommodate 4 to 5 guests.

Year-round availability with heating.

- Houseboat at the Sneekermeer:

Situated directly on the Sneekermeer with a vibrant marina ambiance,.

Ideal for water sports enthusiasts, it offers a beach club with a restaurant.

Unobstructed views of open water and passing boats from large windows.

Suitable for four people with front and back terraces for sunrise or sunset.

Memorable moments watching sailors and diverse water birds.

- Unique Houseboat in Den Bosch:

Inspired by Airstream caravans, blending American classic design with Dutch flair.

Remarkably spacious, accommodating up to 5 people with 2 bedrooms.

Cozy sitting room with a sofa bed, designed for a special night.

Permanent mooring in the water city of's-Hertogenbosch.

Thoughtfully designed inside and out, combining aesthetics with comfort.

- Houseboat with Its Own Slide:

A luxury escape for a couple or a family of four, offering unique experiences.

Features comfortable beds, a terrace for morning dives, and private decks.

Fully equipped kitchenette, bathroom with shower and toilet, and spacious living area.

Aft deck, foredeck, and upper deck with a fantastic view; fun slide for all ages.

Create unforgettable memories in a serene and private houseboat setting.

- Design Houseboat:

A beautifully designed houseboat is located on the water in a unique setting.

Low terrace and large windows for a close connection with water and nature.

Part of an informative and educational center with catering establishments.

Ideal for a unique overnight stay surrounded by natural beauty.

Fully equipped for an extended stay; 2 terraces for enjoying the surroundings.

Explore the charm of the Netherlands with these distinctive houseboat stays, offering a perfect blend of comfort and unforgettable experiences.

C.Countryside Retreats

- Giethoorn, Overijssel:
Experience the tranquility of the "Venice of the North" with charming canals and thatched-roof houses.

- Kinderdijk, South Holland:
Unwind in picturesque Kinderdijk, known for iconic windmills and scenic bike paths along the water.

- Veluwe Region, Gelderland:
Explore the vast Veluwe region, featuring dense forests, heathlands, and Hoge Veluwe National Park.

- Zaanse Schans, North Holland:
Escape to Zaanse Schans for historic windmills, traditional houses, and artisan workshops.

- Gouda Countryside, South Holland:
Discover the peaceful landscapes around Gouda, adorned with meandering rivers and historic villages.

- Limburg's Hill Country:

Retreat to Limburg's rolling hills, vineyards, and charming villages for a relaxed countryside experience.

- Ameland Island, Wadden Sea:

Enjoy the tranquility of Ameland Island, featuring pristine beaches, dunes, and rural landscapes.

- Waterland, North Holland:

Experience the serene Waterland region north of Amsterdam, known for scenic polders and charming villages.

- Drenthe Province:

Unplug in Drenthe's serene countryside, characterized by megalithic structures and picturesque landscapes.

- Texel Island, North Holland:

Escape to Texel, the largest Wadden Island, offering peaceful beaches, dunes, and nature reserves.

- Twente Region, Overijssel:

Retreat to Twente, known for green landscapes, historic estates, and a network of cycling and hiking trails.

- Westhoek Region, Zeeland:

Experience the tranquility of Westhoek in Zeeland, featuring wide-open spaces and charming coastal villages.

The Netherlands"countryside retreats provide an idyllic escape, inviting you to embrace peace, natural beauty, and a slower pace of life away from bustling urban centers. Whether along canals, windmills, or rural villages, these retreats offer a serene getaway.

Chapter Eight

Essential Resources

A. Useful Websites and Apps

Websites

- Visit the Holland Official Website:
Official tourism hub offering insights into attractions, events, and practical travel tips.

- Netherlands Tourism Board:
Explore travel insights, regional information, and cultural highlights.

- NS (Dutch Railways):
Dutch Railways' official site with train schedules, routes, and ticket details.

- 9292 Public Transport Planner:
Plan public transportation routes using trains, buses, and trams.

- Schiphol Airport Official Website:
Amsterdam Airport Schiphol provides flight information and services.

- Amsterdam Visitor's Guide:

Comprehensive tourist guide covering attractions, events, and practical tips.

- Dutch Weather Forecast:

KNMI offers reliable weather forecasts for planning activities.

- Dutch Government Travel Advice:

Official travel advice from the Dutch government for a secure journey.

- Public Transport Card (OV-chipkaart):

Information on the smart card used in the Netherlands' public transport.

- Buienradar (Rain Radar):

Real-time rain radar for accurate weather predictions is crucial in a country with sudden rain.

- Dutch Cycling Routes:

Plan cycling adventures with detailed maps and points of interest.

- Dutch Language Learning Resources:

Duolingo helps you learn basic Dutch phrases and language skills.

- Dutch Healthcare Information:

Healthcare for Expats provides information on health services for travelers.

- Culture Trip Netherlands:

Discover local insights, cultural events, and travel recommendations.

- Dutch News in English:

Stay updated on current events and news in English with DutchNews.

These websites cover diverse aspects, ensuring a seamless and informed experience in the Netherlands, from transportation and weather to cultural exploration and language learning.

Apps

- DigiD:

Simplify governmental processes, from taxes to healthcare, with this digital ID app.

- 112NL:

Emergency app for contacting Dutch authorities; accessible for non-Dutch speakers and those with impairments.

- Google Translate:

Translate Dutch text, including train announcements or grocery labels, with added camera translation.

- Welcome to NL:

A comprehensive relocation app guides you through tasks before, upon arrival, and upon settling in the Netherlands.

- Banking Apps:

Manage your finances on the go, such as with ABN Amro's app, considering the country's debit card preference.

- Tikkie:

Simplify group payments via WhatsApp, making "going Dutch" effortless.

- Buienalarm:

Be weather-ready with real-time rain predictions, a must-have in the Netherlands' unpredictable climate.

- 9292:

Plan your journeys using various modes of public transport, ensuring seamless travel across the country.

- NS (Dutch Railways):

Your go-to app for train-related information, schedules, and ticket purchases.

- Felyx:

Rent e-scooters for quick and affordable transportation, especially in inclement weather.

- Bol.com:

Explore a wide range of products on this popular Dutch webshop with quick delivery options.

- Marktplaats:

Buy or sell used items, from vintage lamps to everyday essentials.

- Thuisbezorgd:

Order food delivery from local restaurants, offering a variety of cuisines.

- Gorillas:

Get groceries delivered quickly to your doorstep with this convenient app.

- Too Good to Go:

Combat food waste by purchasing surprise food packages from local eateries.

- Reclamefolder:

Stay updated on the latest deals and offers from local stores and supermarkets.

- Vinted:

Shop and sell second-hand clothing on this platform, promoting sustainable fashion.

- SweatCoin:

Get paid for walking and use your earnings for various rewards or charitable donations.

- Stocard:

Store all your loyalty cards in one app for easy access during checkout.

- TicketSwap:

Buy and sell event tickets for a variety of activities, offering flexibility for last-minute plans.

Navigate your Dutch experience seamlessly with these apps, covering everything from emergencies to groceries and cultural events.

B. Emergency Contacts

Emergency Services and Key Contacts in the Netherlands

- Emergency Services (112):

Dial 112 for fire, police, or ambulance emergencies. Operators speak English, German, and French.

- Fire Services (Brandweer):

Call 112 for fire emergencies, altitude rescue, and more. Non-emergency situations: 0900–0904.

- Police (Politie):

Emergency: Dial 112. Non-emergency: Call 0900 884 or visit politie.nl. Anonymous crime tips: Meld Misdad Anoniem at 0800 7000.

- Healthcare and Accidents:

Ambulance (112) for emergencies. Contact your GP or find an out-of-hours medical clinic (huisartsenpost) for urgent, non-life-threatening issues.

- National Medical Services Information (0900 1515):

For information on all medical services, please call us 24/7.

- Local Emergency Doctor's Services:

Amsterdam region (SHDA): 088 003 0600

The Hague (SMASH): 070 346 9669

Rotterdam (Rijnmond): 010 290 9888 (south), 010 466 9573 (north-center), 010 279 9262 (east)

Utrecht (Primair Huisartsenposten): 0900 450 1450

Eindhoven, Geldrop, and Helmond (CHP Zuidoost-Brabant): 0900 8861

- Emergency Pharmacies (Dienstapotheek):

Check the Apotheek website with your town or postcode for the nearest out-of-hours pharmacy.

- Dental Emergencies:

Find a dentist online at tandarts.nl, or refer to the guide on emergency dental care in the Netherlands for a list of clinics.

In case of lost documents (passport, ID card, or driving license), contact your embassy before the police. For urgent but non-life-threatening health issues, contact your GP or an out-of-hours medical clinic. For medication outside of opening hours, locate an emergency pharmacy. The provided contact details ensure assistance in various emergency situations in the Netherlands.

C.Packing Essentials

- Weather-Appropriate Clothing:

Pack layers for the variable Dutch weather, including a waterproof jacket and comfortable walking shoes.

- Travel Adapters:

Ensure you have the right power adapters for charging electronic devices in the Netherlands.

- Comfortable Daypack:

Carry a daypack for daily excursions with essentials like water, snacks, a map, and personal items.

- Reusable water bottle:

Stay hydrated on the go with a reusable water bottle, especially if engaging in outdoor activities.

- Travel Documents:

Bring essential documents like a passport, travel insurance, flight tickets, and any required visas.

- Local Currency:

Have some euros for small expenses and places that may not accept credit cards.

- Comfortable Footwear:

Pack comfortable walking shoes for city exploration or countryside adventures.

- Adaptable Power Strip:

Consider an adaptable power strip for charging multiple devices from a single outlet.

- Universal Travel Lock:

Secure your belongings with a universal travel lock for luggage.

- Rain Gear:

Pack a compact rainponcho or travel-sized umbrella for unexpected rain showers.

- Travel-sized Toiletries:

Bring travel-sized toiletries for personal hygiene during your trip.

- Compact Camera or Smartphone:

Capture memories with a compact camera or smartphone with a good camera.

- Reusable shopping bag:

Carry a foldable, reusable shopping bag for souvenirs or items you pick up.

- Guidebook or Maps:

Navigate cities and discover hidden gems with a guidebook or maps.

- Medications and First Aid Kit:

Pack necessary medications and a small first aid kit for minor injuries.

- Travel Pillow and Blanket:

Enhance comfort during flights or long train rides with a travel pillow and blanket.

- Sunscreen and sunglasses:

Protect yourself from the sun with sunscreen and sunglasses for outdoor activities.

- Language Translator App:

Download a language translator app, although English is widely spoken in the Netherlands.

Tailor your packing list based on your itinerary and preferences, ensuring a comfortable and enjoyable trip to the Netherlands, whether you're exploring cities, countryside, or coastal areas.

Conclusion

In 2024, set out on an incredible journey through the Netherlands, a country whose stunning scenery, fascinating history, and lively culture promise to weave an unforgettable tapestry of experiences that will forever alter your travelog. Start your journey in Amsterdam, the vibrant city renowned for its famous canals, ancient buildings, and rich artistic legacy. Admire the intricate beauty of the Anne Frank House, tour the renowned Rijksmuseum, and meander through the quaint streets of Jordaan. As you ride along paths surrounded by trees and take in the eclectic energy of the city, you will truly experience the essence of Dutch culture. Explore the Dutch countryside beyond Amsterdam to find the undiscovered treasures strewn there. In the spring, endless fields of tulips create a kaleidoscope of colors at the famed flower garden, Keukenhof.

Made in United States
Troutdale, OR
04/06/2024

18997692R00080